GOD'S MONEY MYTHOS

GOD'S Conduit to Success

A.B. McCage

GOD'S MONEY MYTHOS

GOD'S CONDUIT TO SUCCESS

BY A.B. MCCAGE

Copyright © 2016 by A.B. MCCAGE

This is a work of fiction. All characters' names, places, and events are the imagination of the author. Any likeness to other books, places, locales, or individuals is by coincidence. Any resemblance to names, businesses, companies, events, or imagery is not intended by the author.

All rights reserved. No part of this publication may be reproduced, distributed, or transmitted in any form or by any means, including photocopying, recording, or other electronic or mechanical methods, without the prior written permission of the publisher, except in the case of brief quotations embodied in critical reviews and certain other noncommercial uses permitted by copyright law.

INTRODUCTION

We are living in very challenging times. It's sometimes hard to remember the abundance of the world. GOD created the world with a set of principles that continue to help us, regardless of the situations we face. The natural laws of the universe still continue unchanged. I don't believe life was meant to be a struggle. Most of us were never taught about our own personal energy and how it connects to everything else in the world. The body we have been given is energy and money is energy. This energy correlates to feelings. These feelings have the power to create reality. These feelings have a spiritual identity, which corresponds to our thoughts. Money possesses this strong earth energy. The feeling of power, success, wealth, abundance and knowing.

There is a divine abundance, which has been given to everyone. We have to align to money and understand the inner game. This book was written to help people understand their hidden power, through a spiritual understanding of money. I believe everyone can be rich, spiritual and wise. The feeling of lack is only a state of mind, which gets in our way. The lack of love, attention, money, health, relationships and other concepts. We suffer from a limited mindset. We must realize, that we are responsible for our own empowerment. This starts in the mind. So take the time to think and put together your plan. Once you start on your plan, the momentum moves to get you closer to what you want.

Let's get right into it. This book is about money consciousness. It was also written to help you help yourself. We must understand, in order to gain wealth. It requires the assistance of other people. No matter how you look at it, every business or individual has acquired wealth by the participation of others. The concept of rich is not just about money. It's about an exchange, which takes place before the money is given. A powerful adjust in the mind from lack to abundance will help you understand this. We will begin with a few definitions and practical concepts.

Practical Concepts

Mythos

A set of beliefs, traditions or assumptions about something; which eventually lead to the truth. A set of stories, writings or conversations, with a significant truth or meaning.

Wealth

An abundance of valuable material possessions or money. It is also considered a plentiful supply of any particular resource.

Real wealth is your time and freedom. This time and freedom is a resource and vibration, which can be termed as an economic energy. We use this time and freedom as a form of trade for money. It happens in the form of physical work at a particular job site. What I call an employee perspective. The main point here is to realize. This places more importance on the physical aspect of money. The physical work which must be done to receive a paycheck. We have just exchanged our energy for a currency, which we deem valuable.

Instead of wanting more time and freedom, to figure out ways to make money. It places you in a never ending cycle of physical work. The freedom to think and time to formulate a worthy idea is more important. This is where the millionaires and billionaires are created. The rich spend more time thinking of ways and ideas to make money. Everything is viewed as an opportunity and not a problem. They nail down a vision or idea, which can help solve a problem or provide a service. Then take action on making that vision real, which later translates into wealth. Every individual on this earth has the same visionary power, which can blossom into millions and billions of dollars. It all depends on how you view yourself and money. It also depends on what you want.

Currency

Currency means to circulate or flow from one hand to the other, one bank to another - the physical exchange of cash or computerized bank record; it must continue to exchange hands to retain some value. Meaning, it has no value without the backing of an institution that can state its value and deem it a form of payment. Its value is determined by the stated or printed numbers on the paper. Its value is later traded for products, goods or services. This is the paper form of currency we place in our wallets. It is also a transference of energy from one place to another.

Money

What is money? Money is physically an item, tool or instrument of influence. It is normally accepted as payment for services, goods or repayment of debt. Its main function is a medium of exchange with a stored value. The thing about money is that it has a stored value. Like gold. It is the same around the world on a per ounce value. Meaning, golds' physical properties don't change. This allows its value to stay constant over a long period of time. So, real money is the gold that backs paper currency. Not the actual paper currency.

Currency values change up and down. It is only determined by the stated or printed numbers on the paper. The paper may be worth ninety eight cents on a dollar one day. Then only five cents on a dollar the next. Gold or money maintains its purchasing power over a longer period of time. In other words, gold is real.

The Future of Money

One more thing before we get to the good stuff. There is a lot of talk about the financial system crashing. The fall of the dollar or the economy collapsing. Whatever, you name it. There may be some truth to the matter. This is an evidence of the constant changes in the value of currency.

The question is, if everything stops and currency no longer circulates. Who loses? The poor lose, because there is no currency in circulation. They are not able to pay bills, buy goods, services or engage in other activities. The rich lose because the circulation of their currency has stopped. Meaning it no longer has any value. It literally becomes equal to toilet paper.

Who will produce the goods and services needed, if money or currency is not circulating? Remember, money is just a byproduct or tool used in the currency system. Known as paper money. Once the system stops, everything stops. So what happens? Currency is pumped back into the economy to keep the circulation going. There must be some type of transference. Energy is never destroyed, just transferred in another direction. This is similar to the body. The body is always in constant circulation. When someone has a heart attack, the blood has been obstructed in some fashion. In order to get the blood circulating again, a current of electricity must shock the heart to get it moving again. Sometimes the arteries have to be unclogged or redirected. This is what happens in the economy. The circulation of money may stop in one direction, but it flows into another. This will happen due to a change or shock in the money system. It happens every thirty to forty years.

We will not be going any deeper here on the basic definition of money. The internet has plenty of definitions to explain the idea of money. Let's move our attention to how it really works and how to control its circulation towards you. This was a quick review of the difference between money and currency.

Multiple Streams of Income

Most of us believe building multiple streams of income will create wealth. There is some truth to this, but let's explore the topic. When most people think or talk about multiple streams of income, they imagine someone having three or four different businesses. I use to think the same thing about multiple streams of income. I had a surface level view, without the details. I started to do research and had an opportunity to speak with several millionaires. I arrived at a different perspective. Let's say you have a job, small business, an internet opportunity and some other income producing activity. At this point you are splitting your energy between four different opportunities. This means you are not focusing all your energy on one thing. If you are only putting in twenty five percent towards each opportunity, you will only get twenty five percent back. This splits up your brain power and your time. There is no way to manage time. Time never stops to allow you to do more. So you can only manage the tasks you perform within twenty four hours.

If you can put all your focus and time into one idea, the possibilities and speed of this idea coming into fruition, increases by the amount of energy you put into it. So don't focus on building separate streams of income. It's harder to get all four streams of income going at the same time. This is why I was not getting the results I wanted. This applies to everything we do. We have to have focused energy to get the results we want. The goal is to pick one idea and push it 100%. If you have a job and want to start a business stay employed and figure out what you want to do. Then do the research on your idea. Utilize a portion of your work income to build your idea. Hopefully at this point, you have some money rolling in from your idea. A second stream of income will show itself.

For example, a singer or songwriter perfects their music skills. As a result of showing their mastery of music on a high level, opportunities open up which allows them to have their music in movies, commercials and other advertisements. Some of them become actors, producers and public speakers. Good examples of this would be Will Smith, Mark Wahlberg and Frank Sinatra. They all started with one idea or activity in mind. This one idea made them famous. Then opened the door to other opportunities or other streams of income.

The universe shows us this by how a tree grows in nature. It starts with one branch sprouting from a seed or idea. Then it focuses a 100% on forming a strong foundation with one branch. This one branch supports all the other branches on the tree. Multiple streams will form off the strength of one branch and grow to support others. The branches can all be traced back to one source.

Let's look at some more examples.

Bill Gates' dream was to put a computer in every home. He focused one hundred percent of his time on completing this task. He put together a Computer Operating Systems called Microsoft. He licensed the system to several different computer manufacturers. Microsoft later became the dominating operating system in the computer industry. It made its way to the majority of home computer systems. Bill's focused attention allowed him to become a pioneer and expert in his industry, which led to the need for operating systems on PDAs, cell phones, tablets and TVs. He was also able to create an XBOX video game console, which runs on his operating system. The strength of one idea or stream of income, leading to other streams of income.

Michael Jordan's dream was to become a basketball player. He focused a hundred percent of his energy on his dream or thoughts of playing basketball. This led to a stream of income as an NBA Professional Basketball Player. This branched off into a shoe deal, clothing, TV commercials and later Brand Jordan.

Focus on one stream and give it one hundred percent of your time. It will lead you to another stream of income. Focused Energy will lead to influence and money!!!!!!!

Chapter One

Perception.

The perception you have about money is what determines how much money comes your way. For example, I always heard the phrase "money is the root of all evil." If you believe money is evil, then why use it to pay for gas, bills, clothing and other products. I would also hear "The love of money is the root of all evil." Then why do you spend forty hours a week in exchange for evil. This is not making any sense. I believe if you are in love with money to a point where you are not able to balance the other pleasures and experiences of life. Then it becomes a problem.

Hebrews 13:5

"Keep your life free from love of money, and be content with what you have, for he has said, I will never leave you nor forsake you."

This means being grateful for what you have. You may want more money, but if you realize that, your desires change. Keep your faith, focus on them and God will grant them as well. So don't fall in love with money to the point where you forsake everything else. The goal is to keep your faith focused on your desires. The desires you have include your time and freedom. When I say desires that also includes your passion, talents, gift, expertise and wisdom. This also includes the thoughts and things you wish to create, which could also bring money into your life. Focusing some time on money is not evil. Spend more time focusing on the product or service you can offer in exchange for money. This is where your focus should be, not just on the physical aspect of money. It becomes so-called "evil" when you focus all your time on its physical nature. This will get in the way of your creativity, which is in the mind. The creativity you receive when you have the time and freedom to think. This is why the rich stay rich. They spend more time thinking of ways to make money; whereas, a large percentage of the population spends their time working and waiting for their next paycheck to come around, in comparison to the rich. We are wasting our time. This is just a different perception to view life. It simply indicates we all have something more to offer, than just our physical abilities. Also realize abundance and wealth, including health, peace of mind and time.

Negative Thought Processes

Stop saying money is evil, you know you don't want evil to come your way. Then you wonder why you never have enough money. It is, because you believe and feel you will never have enough money. The crazy part about it is people spend all their time trying to get something, they don't believe they can have. Why spend your time trying to gain something you don't want. This is what I call wasting time.

This is why rich people don't hang out with poor people. It would compromise the rich person's ideas about money. Most people without money tend to be more judgmental. They judge people based on how much money they have. Instead of trying to figure out what they do for money. Our belief system determines our perspective. If you believe money will make you evil, then it will. If you believe money will make you happy, then it will. I truly think the rich believe working is the absolute worst way to make money. I had to really sit down and challenge my thinking. I was never educated on this point of view. Having this belief system allowed them to look at money from a different perspective. They look for opportunities to create a flow of money. The working class looks for another job. I was tired of going to interviews just to take another job. It may have paid a lot more money, but I still wasn't truly happy or satisfied. I wanted to control my time and earning potential.

This is an example of two different belief systems. Working for money or creating a way for money to flow to you. It's up to you to determine where you want to be. The famous phrase "Fake it until you make it" Most people believe this means act rich. It means encompass the feeling and attitude of whatever you want to do or be. So fake it until your mind and focused energy makes it real. A good way to get the fake it, to you make it attitude flowing.

Purchase a new pair of shoes and clothing, which represent what you want to be. The feeling of something new on your body, allows you to think, feel and act the part. It will allow you to express the energy of what you want.

If you can answer yes to the following questions, the views, thoughts and beliefs you have about money are negatively charged.

1. Do you believe day dreaming will make you poor?
2. Do you believe spending will make you poor and saving will make you rich?
3. Do you believe other people and the economy is why you are in your current situation?
4. Do you believe a good job and profession is the only way to make money?
5. Do you avoid enjoyable spending?
6. The best way to use a bank is to put money in and leave it there?
7. Do you believe there is a limit to how much you can earn?
8. Do you believe there is a difference between you and people with money?

9. Do you believe money earned should only be spent on serious purchases?

The previous questions represent a poverty mindset. This is partially based on what others have told you about money. It's not just the idea of poverty. It places limitations on what your possibilities are. I would like to think that most people who tell us these things mean well. I believe they have accepted their limitations and can only speak on their experiences. Some of us choose big and others choose small. I believe we all have the opportunity to choose big. We just settle for less and use whatever excuse that feels good.

"If you can control a man's thinking you do not have to worry about his action. When you determine what a man shall think you do not have to concern yourself about what he will do. If you make a man feel that he is inferior, you do not have to compel him to accept an inferior status, for he will seek it himself. If you make a man think that he is justly an outcast, you do not have to order him to the back door. He will go without being told; and if there is no back door, his very nature will demand one."

Carter G. Woodson

BELIEFS

Beliefs are thoughts and traditions you repeat in your mind. They can also be repeated through some daily ritual. They could be good or bad. Beliefs create the causes and effects in our lives. This topic is what keeps most of us from what we want. Negative beliefs breed negative results.

For example:

I don't have what I want, because it was not meant for me. Do you think the person who has it, believes it is not for them? There was a middle aged woman who lived in a mansion. She would always say:

"I am tired of paying people to clean this house. I also grow tired of doing the little cleaning I do. One day I will be living in a cardboard box with nothing to clean."

Eight months later she became ill and was not able to care for herself. Her family moved her to an assisted living facility, where she had one small boxed shaped room. She had an employee who cleaned her and her room every day. The universe or GOD granted her wish. She repeatedly focused and believed, then received what she asked for. When you think and speak these negative feelings, the mind accepts the fact that you don't deserve what you have or desire. Everyone wants something. The mind works based on your beliefs and feelings. In exchange, it helps you form your outside world.

One negative belief you must drop, is the something for nothing thought process. The universe or GOD operates based on exchange. The money or currency system operates based on exchange. How will you get something for nothing? There is always an exchange. It may be mental, vibrational or physical. Some may be big, other may be small. Everything that happens in your life starts with a thought. Thoughts become expressed or pressed out into your life. Everything you think, believe and say becomes manifested physically. I had a friend of mine explain to me how a small lie came true.

"The other day a female friend asked me to accompany her to the mall. I didn't want to go, so instead of saying no, I told her my left leg was hurting, so that I could pass on account of not being able to do any walking. The next day I woke up. My left leg was hurting. I was not able to walk for thirty minutes."

This is evidence of how our thoughts control us. He was not aware of how this small lie could manifest into something real. It manifested quickly, because he forgot about it later. This is similar to what self-help gurus refer to imagine and forget. The purpose is to imagine what you want. Then forget about it. The act of forgetting allows it to flow from your mind into the world of reality. If you continue to think about it, it sometimes never leaves your mind. You want your ideas to leave the realm of thought. This is why it is good to write things down. Then review them daily.

The process is to imagine, forget and then take action. All of our experiences in life are some form of our expression of thought. This turns into beliefs. Those beliefs control our thoughts, actions and conditions. These beliefs either good or bad bring forth the fruit of our minds.

"Thy shall know a man by the fruit of his loins."

Literal Bible Acts 2:30

"Being therefore a prophet and knowing that God swore to him with an oath to set out of the fruit of his loins upon his throne."

If you believe and know you can have what you want. Then GOD and the universe will bring it forth. Most of us already know what we want. Start taking action. Sometimes it's a risk, not taking a risk. If you don't take action on something, surely something will take action on you.

A strong, serious belief must come true based on law and principle. The principle of cause and effect. The principle states: "there are no events that happen by chance. All things are caused by a physical or mental event."

Now if we believe in a creator (regardless of your religion) who created the earth and the universe. The creator is the cause and the universe the effect. This is a confirmation of how order or principle controls us. The earth was manifested through the imagination of the creator. So, million dollar ideas are created in the mind. Then manifested through making the idea real or physical. The creator himself had to imagine the universe and all its wonders first. He had to believe he could create something on a large scale. Then he worked six days to make it real. So why would we think something is going to happen without us seeing it in our minds first. The creator had to work on his creation to make it real. So something for nothing equals nothing. We have to work toward our ideas, visions and dreams. The work is first mental, then physical.

This is one of GOD'S laws that always works, regardless of the situation. The creator started the universe through cause and effect. We must use the same process to create our own universe. That's why it is important to protect your thoughts. Things do come true. It depends on what your truth is.

LAW OF GIVING AND RECEIVING

If a hand cannot open to give, how can it be open to receive? If your hand or mind is closed to giving, whether it be money, time, mental capacity or personal belongings, then your hand or mind is closed to receiving these same possibilities. I now understand why millionaires and billionaires give away money. They must open up themselves to receiving by giving. Similar to the principle of cause and effect. If your cup has become full, pour some out, in order to receive more in.

"Presents are made for the pleasure of who gives them, not the merit of who receives them."

Carlos Ruiz Zafon.

**"Prosperity grows by sharing. You can only have more for yourself by giving it away to others."
Unknown**

There is coexistence between living organisms and energy exchange. The earth supplies us with trees, which release oxygen for us to breath. We release carbon dioxide, which is utilized by the trees. There is a constant energy exchange of currency and movement, in terms of money and wealth. Money must be kept in circulation. The action of giving attracts more money. In order for this to work, your intentions must be sincere. Remember, we are dealing with energy. When you decide to give, let it be from your heart and not with ulterior motives to receive. The feelings or energy you release during giving, must be pure of heart. If it is not pure of heart, the energy will return in the same fashion in which it was released.

"Money is like manure, it's not worth a thing unless it's spread around to encourage youthful things to grow." Thornton Wilder.

Ecclesiastes 11: 1-2 (New living Translation)

"Send your grain across the seas, and in time, profits will flow back to you.

But divide your investment among many places, for you do not know what risks might lie ahead."

The first verse is giving and receiving. The second verse refers to multiple streams of income. I already explained that earlier.

Now let's dig a little deeper. The universe operates through constant energy exchange. Every exchange is a push and pull, cause and effect, give and take, giving and receiving. We will use a business as an example. A business or company offers a product or service. The leaders of the company use their own money or borrow money from some source. The money gives the company power to hire employees, purchase materials or set up services to offer to the public. The money has just been exchanged for labor and materials. The finished product or service is offered at a price, which establishes value. Consumers use the money they earn in exchange for this product or service. The business has generated an energy of exchange at a value they determine. The money flows back in as a by-product of the goods and services purchased.

The company had to give before they received. They had to give or offer their service. The objective is to help provide the customer with something, in exchange for money. A constant energy exchange takes place. An employee must constantly come to work to exchange their time for money. So the question is, what's more important, time or money? I explained that earlier in the book. I just wanted to make sure you understand time is money. Will you spend all your time working or creating something you can exchange for money? This will allow you to get the time and freedom you really want. The company opened a channel or conduit for the energy to flow. The money flows in from the service or product sells. Then flows out to employees, materials, the purchase of other services and profit.

Currency means to run or flow. Just like an electrical current running through a house or building. If you plugged up a microwave at your house, it provides you with a service. If you plug it up at the next door neighbors, at work or some building down the street. There must be a current flowing to energize that microwave to service you. Something has to give in order for you to get.

Money symbolizes a current of your own personal energy. This could be the job you have. Any place you exchange personal energy in exchange for an hourly rate. This could also be the business you own, where you determine your time and product of exchange. So how do you determine your worth? It is determined by the degree of influence you have. I will explain degrees of influence later.

Energy can be seen as emotional feelings. Some days you feel good, some days you feel bad. This is determined by your thought patterns. Spend your time feeling good and thinking positively about yourself and money.

In conclusion.

Start experiencing the Law of Giving and Receiving.

Give a gift to anyone you run into. This could be money, a compliment, a prayer or a moment to help. This will get the energy circulating.

Also be a good receiver. Be open to receiving from others. I know sometimes we may not use what we receive. It may not be for you. You are just a conduit for it to flow to someone else.

Silently be happy for other people. A happy feeling with imagination, really gets the energy moving.

Deserving

What if you become what you say you are? Everyone should feel they are deserving. Meaning you should feel, that you can have everything you want! Most people would say that's not possible. The question is, what about the people who have everything they feel they deserve? The difference is the barrier we place on ourselves. If you tell yourself you want to be a millionaire, singer, business owner or top employee. The moment you feel like you deserve it. I mean deserve it to a point where you believe it. That's the moment you move closer to what you want. The process may not be clear on how it will happen. The fact that you believe, moves it into action. The process will come to you on how to make it real. This is why you get around people who are doing what you want to do. The more you become what you want, the closer it gets to you. Fake it until you make it.

Let's dive into the different levels of creation, manifestation and realization.

Spiritual Level

The spiritual level or mental plane of existence. This is where imagination and thought takes place. The place where feelings and emotions begin. The vibrational alignment where your thoughts connect to your feelings. This is where you have to become comfortable with what you want and know you deserve it. Don't just think you do, know you do. It's very important to move from thinking to knowing. This helps produce and fulfill your beliefs. It's not just what you think. It's the way you think.

Let's take a more in depth look. Most people want more money. Their wants need to be cultivated here. If the negative feelings or doubts about money exist here, the ideas you have about money will be neutralized. For example, "I want to be a millionaire, but I know I will never have it." The second line neutralizes what you want and deserve. The trick is to align with what you want continuously without deflecting it. In other words, stop getting in your own way.

"I AM a millionaire, because I know, I can have it and deserve it." There is no resistance in this statement.

Remember money is a stream of energy or currency flowing or circulating. Negative feelings create a blockage in the channel or circulation of money to you. This works the same with relationships, marriage, work, business and life. The spiritual aspect deals with the thoughts and vibration you give off concerning any subject. If you say or believe your children are bad and always getting into trouble, then you get more of what you feel and say. You also have to deal with how your thoughts affect their thinking process. Also remove the idea that money is only connected to physical things. Money's energy flows unseen on the spiritual level. One last point. The emotional, personal and psychological feelings you have. Reflect on how you use and deal with your money.

Psychic level

This is where feelings and emotions reside. This is the non-material ideas that people have, including beliefs, values, rules, morals and norms. For example, religion is a set of ideas and beliefs which determine how people act, live and deal with issues. These concepts shape your thoughts, feelings and emotions. All of this comes together as the mental decisions we make. The feeling is the key. We make decision based on how we feel. You must feel the energy of money. It is close to the feeling of love. This is why negative thought processes, reflect money. Money is the lovely feeling of believing you can have it. The thoughts you have can be expressed as a feeling. The feeling is expressed in the subconscious mind, which allows it to manifest on the physical or material level.

The psychic level deals with the feeling of energy and money. I know there are people who have money with bad attitudes. The key we don't realize is, when it comes to the subject of money, they know they can have it and feel they deserve it. They feel good and have positive feelings toward money. They may not feel the same about people, relationships and other aspects of their lives.

MATERIAL LEVEL

The material encompasses the physical objects or resources we use to define ourselves. The physical things define our behaviors and perspectives. The money, houses, cars, clothes and any other physical object. Most people get hung up here. Their experience with money is strictly physical. They will never correlate the $5000 dollars, they saved on the price of a new car, house or vacation; as the energy of money, which spiritually circulated in their favor. We feel good about paying the reduced price. Who doesn't feel good after they believe a deal was made. This is a spiritual exchange of money. No physical exchange took place. The difference between the original price and the reduced price can be viewed as a spiritual flow of energy in your direction. It's funny how you just happened to catch up with what you wanted at a reduced price. I guess you were lucky. Maybe you thought about what you wanted and got the energy moving in your direction. Hm.....The world works in mysterious ways. Moving on.

The process starts with the spiritual imagination or thought; which is transformed into a feeling on the psychic level and moves to an expressed or realized object at the material level.

MEDITATION

Meditation is a practice where an individual can take control of their mind. It allows the person to induce a level of consciousness. It helps us understand our own mind. We can change our negative thoughts to positive thoughts during a single meditation session. How do you meditate? Find a comfortable place to sit. Close your eyes and relax. Make no effort to control your breath. Try to focus on relaxing and let everything go. Focus on something simple at first, start with a red apple. Focus on how it tastes, looks and smell. If your mind wanders, simply focus back on the apple. The goal is to learn to control your mind and thoughts. Once you have more control over your mind, meditate on the desires and goals you have. The mind will start to give you small ideas and visions. These ideas will lead you to discover things you can do to help realize your desire. You will be amazed at the ideas which come to light. This is where that million dollar idea, perfect relationship, career and talents are realized. The goal is to really visualize what you want. The trick is to control your imagination and thought, where you completely focus on that one dominate thought. That one desire you really want, without question. It gives you clues to how you can achieve it. We need to take time to meditate and imagine so we can, feel and allow the energy to flow. This energy is your money. Clear the mind, meditate, and focus on what you really want. The mind will tell you what actions to take.

GODS LAWS AND PRINCPLES

The Law of Divine Oneness: All is energy and connected to everything else. Everything we do, think, say and believe affects everyone else around us. We are all connected to the source known as the universe or GOD.

The Law of Vibration: Each thought, feeling, action and belief, all have a unique vibration. These vibrations create motion. The motion moves in a circular pattern. These patterns come back to us good or back. The vibrations are caused by the thoughts and feelings inside our minds. This leads to corresponding actions in our reality in the physical world.

The Law of Action: Action is energy in motion. We must work towards our goals, desires and wants. By performing actions or tasks that line up with our goals.

The Law of Correspondence: What happens on the inside reflects what happens on the outside. If you think negative things, you bring negative actions or reality into your life. That means if you always feel stressed out, this feeling on the inside will create a situation that corresponds with the outside world. A lot of times we ask, why does this thing or situation keep happening to me? It's a result of our thoughts and feelings. These thoughts and feelings may be dumped on us by our friends and family. We have conversations with people who dump all their negative baggage onto us. We encompass their feelings in an attempt to be understanding and relate. This sometimes changes our thoughts and moods. We start to spend time thinking about their issues. Then their thoughts and situations start to show up in our own personal life. Misery loves company. The company, which vibrates on the same level it is at.

Now you realize how important it is to protect what you allow in your mind. This is why people who want to learn how to deep sea dive, get around people who deep sea dive. People who want to become millionaires, get around people who are millionaires. People who want to learn how to program computers, sign up for computer classes and hang around computer programmers. Think about what you want and hang around people who are already doing it. If you think positive things, positive events will keep coming into your life.

The Law of Cause and Effect: Every action has a corresponding reaction. If you believe you are successful and take successful actions. The end result would have to be success.

The Law of Compensation: This is a sub law of cause and effect applied to abundance, prosperity and wealth. The good that we do comes back to us in different forms matching our energy. Simply put, if you want to increase your compensation, the contribution of energy you expel must match. To receive more you must give more. This applies to money and the energy you put into something. The most common contribution is giving ten percent. The unknown secret is to give fifty percent. This may seem difficult to some. If you watch how millionaires and billionaires give away money, they never really say ten percent. They give half away of a predetermined amount. This is the law of compensation. We are compensated in direct proportion to what we put out. So the energy we put out comes back with equal value. Compensation could be money, material possessions, friendships, relationships, experiences and any other thing you believe or expect.

Law of Attraction: Negative energy attracts negative things. Positive energy attracts positive things.

Law of Transmutation of Energy: We all have the power to change our situations at any given time. Negative energy can be changed to positive energy at any given time.

The Law of Belief: The law firmly states, whatever you believe, think and feel dictates your reality. Our world is made by what we believe is true.

Matthew 8:13

"Then Jesus said to the Roman officer, "Go back home. Because you believed, it has happened." And the young servant was healed that same hour."

Mark 9:23

"What do you mean, 'If I can'?" Jesus asked. "Anything is possible if a person believes."

THE LAW OF THE MIND

The mind is a magnet. What you focus on expands. The subconscious mind responds to mental images. The images can come from inside or from the external world. A single thought may not show its effect. A habit of repeated thoughts will manifest, either good or bad. A repeated thought of failure or fear will never lead to a reality of success. The mind works to fulfill the programmed image it receives. It does not differentiate between reality and imagined thoughts. The thoughts we have affect our emotions, which affect our bodies. If you always worry and have constant fear, this can develop into ulcers in the stomach. The energy of the mind flows out as emotions, which manifest in reality.

The mind has the power to make you poor, sick, happy and successful. This proves that the mind's imagination is more powerful than anything you can learn. So, the longer an idea remains in the mind as an image, the more it becomes a habitual thought. The thought takes on an emotion, which pushes closer to reality. This same habitual thought controls our behavior. The mind learns through repeated thoughts and imagery. It replaces old thoughts, by the repeated imagery of new ones. So change your negative beliefs, by replacing them with repeated positive beliefs.

THE REAL SECRET

Wealth is generated by the assistance or help of others. Every millionaire or billionaire has gained their wealth through the process of participation of others. It may be directly or indirectly. The idea of supply and demand is a twisted concept. Interest and fulfillment is the law. Money is a byproduct of this law. The concept of interest and fulfillment is the willingness of others to participate in an exchange. This is the power that you have. An individual is interested in a product or service, which someone or entity fulfills. (This is done by evoking an emotional response inside of an individual.) One gains a service not money.

For example, in business there is a group of people who agree to participate in an idea, product or service. This would make them employees. Their willingness to participate, gains them a channel of exchange. This exchange is labor or time for money. The company does not gain money. They gain a service from their employees. This same idea, product or service can be offered to the public. The willing participants become the public. They are interested in the product, idea or service in exchange for their money. The company ends with a profit termed money. The public gain a service. Money is still a byproduct of the service.

Now this really gives the business or individual influence which is also power. This influence is used by the company or individual to control the participants involved. So the participants agree to exchange their personal money for the company's influence or perceived product. The main point is, if you are an individual or business trying to make more money the goal is to create an influence that fosters the exchange of money. That's why you don't do things for money. Do it for the influence by way of an idea, product or service. The company gained the power of influence over willing participants.

Business is maintained by this same group of individuals, who agreed to continue to participate. Money is a unit of measure of influence. Let's say you need to purchase a cell phone. There are several different cell phone providers. As a consumer, you will measure the service verses the price. Once you decide the degree of service you need, you will choose the company whose influence matches up closely to your desire. They gain power over you once you pay and participant in their service. This power increases every month, as long as you feel their degree of influence is worth it. Making you a willing participant.

If you didn't catch the explanation, here is another way to view it. If money is given to a man by way of work or profits from a business, he is put in a position to be exploited by those who have influence. The company with influence is the Light Company, Gas Company, Phone Company and Bank. We pay for lights, gas, phone, car note and mortgage. An individual can only obtain these things through the power of what he earns. Your buying power is based on how much influence you can afford.

Profits are not given to people who work or exchange labor for money. They are the makers of profit. They are owned until someone else willingly fulfills their desires. Money is only a token for services rendered. Profit is only given to the owner or company who fulfills the services rendered. This is at the price they determine for their product. So, money is a byproduct or form of payment, for services rendered. Hm.... Sales people and good communicators are some of the highest paid professions. They are good salesman or influencers of a product or service, which could be good or bad. The thing to remember, you agreed to participate.

Poverty is not a lack of money, but a greater amount of obligation. One must do more when he has less. So money is really a unit of measure determined by an individuals' or business' influence.

How do you create influence? What do you have to offer? A friend of mine just happened to be a good singer. He was asked to perform at a wedding. He would always complain about not having enough money. I advised him to sell himself. I advised him to make business cards and sell his service of singing at events. He was not able to imagine it in his mind. A few weeks later he called and explained. He could see himself singing at all kinds of events. He fell asleep one night in a slight meditation and had a dream of singing at different places. Once he saw it in his mind; he made a decision to move forward with his dream. He printed those business cards, set up a Facebook with recorded videos of him singing. Three months later he was earning more money in a week, compared to the forty hours he put in on his job. That fact that he was able to provide a good service, gave him a degree of influence. He later increased his degree of influence by offering singing lessons at an hourly rate he determined. The singing lesson can later be packaged into an online course or CD. Now you can make money while you sleep. He has just established multiple streams of income. He has offered his services, produced a product and packaged it as a tangible good. If you have a good product or service, people will find you and agree to participate. They will then exchange their money for your service.

Wealth comes through varying degrees of influence. His wealth and influence increased by taking control of his time and freedom. A clear mind with a little meditation or visualization will help you find your degree of influence. Some of us already know what our influence is. We just have to act. The main goal is to multiply your same forty hours a week; which will foster several degrees of influence.

Let's say you have a forty hour a week job. That is one form of income. If you started a business, it would be a second form of income. If you offered a product or service for sale online, that's a third source of income. The third source of income operates 24/7 and continually generates residual income. Remember to start with one idea and focus on it one hundred percent. The second and the third will show themselves later. Remember your point of view determines your financial life.

The Process

The process is the most important part of bringing anything into your life.

How to change your thoughts.

STEP ONE

Mind Dump

This is where you eliminate and release all negative thoughts. Get a piece of paper and write down all fear, doubt, worry, concerns, stress and indifference. Write down any reference to money, work, relationships, children, wife and husband. Anything that's on your mind that you need to release. The process of writing it down helps transfer it from your mind to the paper. Then you can burn the paper or throw it away. This helps empty your mind. It will help you feel better to get those thoughts out. Then you can focus on putting what you want in your mind.

Examples:

I forgot to do something for a friend………

I feel bad today about…………

I feel concerned about…………

A second way to complete this process is to imagine a garbage dumpster in your mind. Imagine you were putting everything you wrote down into this dumpster. Then close the lid and visually see it being taken away.

STEP TWO

THINK & FEEL

Think about what you want. Truly open your heart to what you really want. Try to focus on one thing. This process can be repeated for everything else. Whether it be money, a relationship, career, or love, get a clear picture in your mind. Then try to feel it, taste it, smell it and hear it. Steve Jobs' idea for the iPhone came from his mind. He saw it in his imagination first. Then he envisioned saw how it would help people in exchange for money. We all have the same thinking power. Our minds have been focusing on everyday mundane life. We spend too much time on Facebook, watching TV and wasting time. We spend most of our time in survival mode. Just living for the weekend and paying bills. The release from the Mind Dump helps us get rid of the unwanted thoughts. Thoughts placed in our minds from TV commercials, the internet and everyday life.

For example, a popular fast food establishment can run TV commercials during your favorite show. This same commercial plays repeatedly, while you wait for the programming to resume. The next time you get hungry, you decide to eat at that same fast food establishment. Now you know why. Marketing and advertising are fighting for space in your mind. They do this through imagery, which is repeated constantly. The same imagery you need to use for yourself. So see yourself from within your own mind. Imagine what you want, not what they want you to think. Allow visualization to be used for you, not against you. Repeatedly see the image of yourself you want to see.

The "I" in Imagination is the creative power and energy of the universe. The AM as in "I AM" is the action or power of focused energy, which works to bring things into existence. That's why it has to happen in the mind first. So the affirmation:

I AM ……. Allows you to be and become whoever you say you are.

I AM Rich. (Means I AM Rich, in health, love, money, relationship and success.)

I AM healthy.

I AM prosperous.

I AM successful.

Don't worry about the how. Once you start the process more ideas come and doors open. To get you closer to what you want. You have to focus on your desire every day.

STEP THREE

WRITE

Back to the paper to empower your intentions. Write down what you want. Write that dream or idea you always wanted to achieve, then speak it out loud. Write down how much money you want, then speak it out loud. Describe your vision out loud while you visualize it. A good idea is to record yourself speaking your intention. Then play it back every morning and before you go to sleep.

It's been proven that we dream about the last thing we put into our minds. It could be a TV program or conversation that you had before going to bed. It could also be anything that made a serious impression on the mind. Things, people and places show up in our dreams because they are familiar to us. People normally dream about friends or family members. These people show up because we can relate to them in some fashion. The key is to look past the familiarity and figure out what you are supposed to get from the dream.

Write in a journal or a single piece of paper, the ultimate dream, idea, want and desire you have.

It must be detailed and specific. Don't just say I want a lot of money or a good relationship. Get right to the point.

Examples

Car Vision

I want a white Mercedes-Benz S Class, two door convertible. It has black interior, stick shift with three hundred and fifty horse power. I can feel the rivets on the back of the steering wheel with my left hand. I depress the brake with my left foot and shift into second gear while making a right turn. I can feel the suns' rays on the back of my neck. The wind is blowing through my hair as I speed down the expressway. The song by Pharrell "I am happy" plays through the speaker, as I pull up to a parking space at the beach.

This is the specificity that GOD and the universe want.

I had a friend of mine tell me he wanted to win the lottery. He played and won a dollar the next day. He wanted to know how to get to the real money. I said a dollar is real in your hand and pocket. He said yes. Will one million dollars be real in your hand and in your pocket? He said no. It's what you consider money. So you only believe the real money must fit into your pocket. He said yes. Then you really have some limiting beliefs. How can you get to the so call big money if you can't see yourself with it? Now you know why you can't get to the big money. Your money story needs to be as detailed as the car vision above. The key to winning the lottery. An individual must evoke a powerful vision and feeling; that expresses itself from the spiritual level, to the psychic level and finally to the material level.

Money Vision

I am rich. I am wealthy. I have five hundred thousand dollars in my personal bank account. I woke up this morning and took a shower. I put on my blue polo shirt, khaki shorts and my favorite flip flops. I went downstairs and opened the living room window. The sun was shining and the wind was blowing. I could smell the flowers outside. I sat down and turned on my laptop. I logged into my bank account and observed a half a million dollars. I transferred five thousand dollars from my saving to checking account. I loaded up the family and we headed to Disney world for a two week vacation.

Please be very detailed.

Relationship/Love

I value a relationship with someone who has tolerance, peace, patience's and purpose at the center of their relationship. Someone who is committed to self-development and willing to grow as an individual. A person I can laugh with, have fun with, travel with and enjoy. We stay physically fit, workout together and enjoy sex. Someone I can work with through anger, disagreements and misunderstandings. A person who enjoys their career, understands responsibilities and financial matters. Someone I can trust, spend private time with, feel safe around and have similar political views. Someone who understands and supports my spiritual beliefs.

(The questions is: Are you loveable and do you know what makes you happy? Then you must be able to explain this to your partner.)

Meditation

Now, after writing down what you want, meditate on it. See it. Then decide on it. Most importantly believe it. Get it in your mind, before you can get it in your hand. During meditation feel it to a point where it's expressed as an emotion. The goal is to put an emotional feeling around that thought. The feeling helps impress your thought upon the subconscious mind. The subconscious mind then works to make it a reality.

STEP FOUR

Release it to the unseen world.

Once you have your dreams, desires, goals and visualization written down exactly how you want and feel. Purchase a white candle. Place it in a candle holder or between both hands. If you have a candle holder, place your hand around it. Light the candle. This represents that beacon of light GOD and the universe has already given you. Close your eyes and focus on the vision you wrote down. Really see it clearly in your mind. Then imagine a ball of light around that vision. This is giving that idea a positive charge. This may take a few moments. See that light growing bigger around your vision. Allow it to grow until it encompasses your entire body. Then open your eyes and direct the ball of light into the candle flame. Truly see the light travel down both of your arms into the flame. Allow a few minutes to focus the vision into the flame. Then place the candle in a safe place where it can burn completely out. The goal here is to take the hidden vision in your mind to a physical state of existences. The flame represents your intention. As the flame burns, your intention is being released.

That's it, you are done. The vision is in the universe. It will begin working its way to you physically. Why? The candle and your intention is the cause. There must be an effect. The law says so. This happens every day. We just never take control of the outcome. We normally say "Whatever happens will happen". No more time wasted on that. We have just influenced the outcome. Make sure you believe it will come. If not you are neutralizing everything you have just done.

THE MISSING STEP

The Most Important Step.

Create a conduit. A conduit is a natural or artificial channel through which something is conveyed. It's a means of transmitting or distributing money, information, or products. This is a channel or a current of exchange, for money to come your way. During meditation a perfect idea, will show itself. The idea may also come during your everyday activity. Focus on how you will get it out to the people in exchange for money. Figure out what type of payment system you will use to bring in money. If you have a great product, people will buy.

The law of attraction is not about waiting for things to come to you. It's about taking advantage of opportunities on the path to your desire. Some people already have an idea of what they can do. They have not taken any action on their vision. For example, if you know how to play the piano, set up an opportunity for you to teach piano to others. Set yourself up as a business and have the ability to receive payments.

If you have ten years of experience as a financial expert, figure out a way to offer your services to the public. Exchange your knowledge, which is influence to help someone who needs it. This would be your channel to exchange money for services. Find an online opportunity you feel you can sell. Something you truly and really believe in. Think about how it helps others and how you can exchange it for profit. Remember profit is only made by the business who can exchange a product or service. What we don't realize is everyone is in business for themselves. The rich people have a real understanding of this. We sell ourselves every day, either as a business owner or an individual in exchange of an hourly rate. This is called looking for a job and accepting what's out there. Now change your thought process and go do the job. Now you can control your hours and how much you can make.

Raise your mental consciousness in order to raise your level of thinking. Million dollar ideas will be attracted into your life. Will you be willing to chase them? Remember these ideas come through the process of meditation, realization, belief and feelings. Sounds like you need some quiet time to yourself.

If you get the opportunity to speak with a millionaire, ask them how much it cost to chase a dream. Like I mentioned before, Michael Jordan chased a dream. I believe the dream was worth billions.

Not bad for a one chapter book. The goal was not to give you two to five hundred pages, of stuff you don't understand. The goal is to get you rolling on real information and real things. I wanted it to be easy and simple.

GOD'S MONEY MYTHOS $ 47

MIND DUMP WORKSHEET.

I Feel

I Release.... All Fear

- List Fears

I Release.... All Doubt

- List Doubts

I Release .... All Pain/Blockage/ I Forgive......

- Physical & Mental

I Now DUMP All Unwanted Thoughts, Images, Visions and Feelings

GOD'S MONEY MYTHOS $ 48

GOD'S MONEY MYTHOS $ 49

MIND INPUT

I AM
_____

I BELIEVE
_____

I LOVE
_____

I KNOW
_____

I AM A VALUABLE INCOME PRODUCING INDIVIDUAL. MY SERVICES HELP OTHERS.

I AM GRATEFUL FOR:
_____
_____
_____
_____
_____

CURRENT GIFTS, TALENTS AND EXPERTISE. (USE WHAT EVERY SKILL YOU HAVE OR LOVE AS A CONDUIT.)
_____
_____
_____
_____
_____

GOD'S MONEY MYTHOS $ 50

_____
_____

CLEAR AND SPECIFIC VISION, DESIRES, WANTS.

_____
_____
_____
_____
_____
_____
_____
_____
_____
_____
_____

WHAT IS YOUR *CONDUIT* OF SUCCESS? (WHAT WILL YOU OFFER IN EXCHANGE FOR MONEY? WHAT NEED, PRODUCT OR SERVICE? (THE PRODUCT DOES NOT HAVE TO BELONG TO YOU.)

_____
_____
_____
_____
_____
_____

GOD'S MONEY MYTHOS $ 51

ACHIEVE YOUR DESIRES

What is the one desire you want to achieve.

_____
_____
_____
_____
_____
_____
_____

What will you be offering in exchange. (Product or Service).

_____
_____
_____
_____
_____
_____
_____

How will you exchange your idea, thought, product, service or desire?

_____
_____
_____
_____
_____
_____
_____

You must believe it and never doubt it.

What are the tasks you need to perform every day to get closer to the reality you want?

THE WHY

I look at this every day when I wake up. I know today is the day, I get closer to what I want. I also created a vision board on my computer. I printed out this vision board to look at it every day. It reminds me of why I get up and do what I am doing. I look at the task list to remind me of what I am supposed to do today. The people I need to call. The paperwork I need to set up and complete. The repeated thoughts and reminders help build and create your reality. This is the WHY. This is why your boss constantly preaches company policy and rules. This is why you go through repeated training at work. This is why a business repeats the same process to get the same result. Repetition locks it into the mind. They know the mind learns and acts on repeated messages. This repetition generates an energy, which produces a manifested result.

HAPPINESS, LOVE, SUCCESS, HEALTH AND A WHOLE LOT OF MONEY!!!!!!!!!!!!!
HAPPINESS, LOVE, SUCCESS, HEALTH AND A WHOLE LOT OF MONEY!!!!!!!!!!!!!
HAPPINESS, LOVE, SUCCESS, HEALTH AND A WHOLE LOT OF MONEY!!!!!!!!!!!!!
HAPPINESS, LOVE, SUCCESS, HEALTH AND A WHOLE LOT OF MONEY!!!!!!!!!!!!!
HAPPINESS, LOVE, SUCCESS, HEALTH AND A WHOLE LOT OF MONEY!!!!!!!!!!!!!
HAPPINESS, LOVE, SUCCESS, HEALTH AND A WHOLE LOT OF MONEY!!!!!!!!!!!!!
HAPPINESS, LOVE, SUCCESS, HEALTH AND A WHOLE LOT OF MONEY!!!!!!!!!!!!!

HAPPINESS, LOVE, SUCCESS, HEALTH AND A WHOLE LOT OF MONEY!!!!!!!!!!!!!
HAPPINESS, LOVE, SUCCESS, HEALTH AND A WHOLE LOT OF MONEY!!!!!!!!!!!!!
HAPPINESS, LOVE, SUCCESS, HEALTH AND A WHOLE LOT OF MONEY!!!!!!!!!!!!!
HAPPINESS, LOVE, SUCCESS, HEALTH AND A WHOLE LOT OF MONEY!!!!!!!!!!!!!
HAPPINESS, LOVE, SUCCESS, HEALTH AND A WHOLE LOT OF MONEY!!!!!!!!!!!!!
HAPPINESS, LOVE, SUCCESS, HEALTH AND A WHOLE LOT OF MONEY!!!!!!!!!!!!!
HAPPINESS, LOVE, SUCCESS, HEALTH AND A WHOLE LOT OF MONEY!!!!!!!!!!!!!
HAPPINESS, LOVE, SUCCESS, HEALTH AND A WHOLE LOT OF MONEY!!!!!!!!!!!!!
HAPPINESS, LOVE, SUCCESS, HEALTH AND A WHOLE LOT OF MONEY!!!!!!!!!!!!!

General Information and Questions: ABMcCage@gmail.com

Also join the Email list to receive weekly updates and tips.

I will also be sending out three free eBooks to help you on your journey. Email me at: ABMcCage@gmail.com   Please put "3 free eBooks" in the subject line.

Please join me on facebook: www.facebook.com/GODSMoneyMythos

YouTube Channel: "GODS Money Mythos" Great video's

Part two of the book will be an Audio Component, which is on the YouTube channel.

Thank You for your purchase and if the book helped or inspired you. Please leave a positive review.

www.ingramcontent.com/pod-product-compliance
Lightning Source LLC
Chambersburg PA
CBHW070401190526
45169CB00003B/1064